Guide to LangChainJS

Practical Guide

V. Telman

Copyright © 2024

Practical Guide

1.Introduction

LangChainJS is one of the implementations of the LangChain framework, designed for use with large language models (LLMs). LangChain has become a popular tool for building AI-based applications because it simplifies the development process of systems that leverage language models to perform various tasks, such as text generation, question answering, classification, and more. With the growing demand for AI tools in JavaScript, LangChainJS is an excellent solution for integrating the power of language models into web or Node.js applications. In this guide, we'll explore what LangChainJS is, its main advantages, and how to install and configure it.

What is LangChainJS?

LangChainJS is a JavaScript library designed to facilitate the development of AI-based applications that leverage language models.

Derived from the broader LangChain framework, LangChainJS is distinguished by its compatibility with the JavaScript environment, making it easier for web and Node.js developers to integrate and orchestrate LLMs in various application contexts.

LangChain's primary goal is to help developers build chains of operations (hence the name "Chain") that involve language models, simplifying interactions with these powerful neural networks. LangChainJS provides tools and abstractions that make it easy to connect LLMs to data sources, orchestrate complex conversations, automate text generation processes, and much more.

The library offers various built-in features that allow developers to efficiently manage inputs and outputs from language models, orchestrate data flows between different components, and integrate third-party models such as OpenAI GPT, Hugging Face, and other AI platforms.

Key Components of LangChainJS

LangChainJS is built around several key components that are combined to create custom AI workflows. Here are some of the main components:

1. **Chains**: A chain is a sequence of operations that processes input, interacts with a language model, and produces an output. LangChainJS offers support for creating simple or complex chains to orchestrate language models and other functions together.

2. **Prompts**: The prompt is the request or input given to the language model. LangChainJS provides tools to effectively build and manage prompts, allowing you to structure complex or chained requests based on the workflow.

3. **LLM (Large Language Models)**: These are large language models such as GPT,

BERT, or Hugging Face models. LangChainJS supports integration with various model providers and allows developers to choose the most suitable model for their applications.

4. **Memory**: Memory enables applications to remember the state of a conversation or process, making it possible to handle dialogues or chains of operations that span multiple steps. This feature is particularly useful in conversational applications, where past context is crucial.

5. **Agents**: Agents in LangChainJS are entities that use language models to perform a series of actions. Agents can receive input, consult external tools or APIs, and generate a final output. These are particularly useful in applications requiring complex user interactions or interactions with other resources.

6. **Tooling**: LangChainJS supports a

range of external tools that can be used by agents or chains. These tools include external APIs, databases, or local resources that agents can consult to enrich the decision-making process.

Key Features and Benefits

LangChainJS offers a variety of advantages for developers looking to integrate language models into their applications. Below are some of the main benefits and features:

1. **Modular Abstractions**: LangChainJS organizes its core components into a modular architecture, allowing developers to use only the components they need and easily customize their AI applications. Chains can be simple or complex, depending on the application's requirements.

2. **Context and Memory Management**: Managing context is one of the main

challenges when working with language models. LangChainJS provides native support for memory, enabling the retention of context across multiple interactions. This is essential for conversational applications or multi-step workflows.

3. **Easy Integration with External Models**: LangChainJS is compatible with various language model providers, including OpenAI, Hugging Face, and other models available via API. This makes it easy to switch or upgrade the model being used without altering the core architecture of the application.

4. **Support for Complex Conversations**: With its context management and agent capabilities, LangChainJS can be used to build advanced conversational applications. This includes chatbots that can remember previous information or applications that require deep question-and-answer processes.

5. **Integrated Tooling**: Agents can consult external tools such as APIs, databases, or other resources, enabling LangChainJS applications to perform complex tasks that require external input in addition to user-provided input.

6. **Extended Ecosystem**: As part of the broader LangChain ecosystem, LangChainJS users benefit from continuous updates, new features, and a large support community. Best practices, code examples, and tutorials are available to help developers get started and improve their projects.

Installation and Configuration

Installing LangChainJS is relatively straightforward and can be done using common JavaScript package managers such as `npm` or `yarn`. Before proceeding with the installation, it's essential to ensure that your system meets the necessary requirements to run the library.

System Requirements

Before installing LangChainJS, ensure that your system meets the following requirements:

1. **Node.js**: LangChainJS requires Node.js version 14 or higher. You can download and install Node.js from the official site nodejs.org.

2. **NPM or Yarn**: LangChainJS can be installed using the NPM package manager (included with Node.js) or Yarn. It's recommended to use the latest version of either package manager.

3. **Internet Connection**: During installation, LangChainJS will download additional packages, and if you plan to use external models such as OpenAI, a stable internet connection will be required.

Installing via npm or yarn

Once the system requirements are met, installing LangChainJS is simple and straightforward. Here are the steps to install the library using `npm` or `yarn`.

1. **Installation via npm**:

   To install LangChainJS using npm, run the following command in your terminal:

   ```bash

   npm install langchain

   ```

2. **Installation via yarn**:

If you prefer to use yarn as your package manager, you can install LangChainJS with the command:

```bash
yarn add langchain
```

Environment Setup

After installing LangChainJS, the next step is to configure your environment to start using it. This may include setting up API keys if you plan to use external models like OpenAI and creating basic scripts or configurations to start working with chains.

1. **Setting up API Keys**:

If you're using a language model provider like OpenAI or Hugging Face, you will need to configure API keys to access their services. For example, to use OpenAI models, you can save your API key in an environment variable:

```bash
export OPENAI_API_KEY=your-api-key
```

In your code, you can then securely access this API key and use it to interact with the models.

2. **Creating a Basic Chain**:

Once the environment is set up, you can start creating your first "chain." Here's an example of a simple chain that uses an OpenAI model to generate text:

```javascript
```

```
const { OpenAI } =
require('langchain/llms/openai');

const llm = new OpenAI({
  apiKey: process.env.OPENAI_API_KEY,
  temperature: 0.7,
});

async function generateResponse(prompt) {
  const response = await llm.generate(prompt);
  console.log(response.text);
}

generateResponse("Write an introduction about LangChainJS.");
```

In this example, we've created a simple

chain that uses an OpenAI model to respond to a text prompt. The model is configured with a `temperature` parameter to control the variability of the generated responses.

3. **Testing the Environment**:

Once the environment is configured and the first script is created, you can run your project with Node.js to test that everything works correctly:

```bash
node your-script.js
```

If everything is set up correctly, you should see a response generated by the language model in the terminal console.

2. Fundamental Concepts

LangChainJS is a versatile library designed to work with language models (LLMs) in the context of JavaScript applications. Built to provide a flexible architecture, it allows developers to orchestrate chains of operations using language models, external tools, and memory, making it an ideal solution for building complex AI applications. In this section, we will explore the fundamental concepts of LangChainJS in detail, including its architecture, key components, and basic workflow.

LangChainJS Architecture

The architecture of LangChainJS is centered around the concept of **chains**, which orchestrate the interaction between language models, context management, and the use of external tools. This modular structure enables developers to build complex AI applications while maintaining flexibility and scalability.

LangChainJS can be divided into several key components, each designed to perform a specific task within a chain of operations. These components can be used in isolation or combined into more complex chains to solve advanced problems. The flexible architecture also allows integration with third-party language models, external APIs, and memory management for maintaining operational context.

Here are the main layers of the LangChainJS architecture:

1. **Chains**

Chains are the core of LangChainJS's architecture. A chain is a workflow that connects inputs, language models, external tools, and outputs. Chains can be configured to perform simple operations, such as answering direct questions, or more complex tasks that require multiple steps.

Example of a simple chain:

```javascript
const { OpenAI } = require('langchain/llms/openai');
const { LLMChain } = require('langchain/chains');

// Set up the OpenAI model
const llm = new OpenAI({
  apiKey: process.env.OPENAI_API_KEY,
  temperature: 0.7,
});

// Create a simple chain to answer a question
const chain = new LLMChain({
  llm: llm,
  prompt: "What is the meaning of life?",
```

```
});

// Execute the chain
async function executeChain() {
  const result = await chain.call();
  console.log(result.text);
}

executeChain();
```

2. **Language Models (LLMs)**

Language models are key components in LangChainJS. These models, such as OpenAI GPT or Hugging Face Transformers, are used to generate text, answer questions, or perform text transformation tasks. LangChainJS supports various LLM providers, allowing you to choose the model that best suits your needs.

LangChainJS allows configuration of language models with parameters such as temperature, which controls the variability of the generated responses, and the token limit, which sets the maximum length of the output.

Example of configuring an LLM with OpenAI:

```javascript
const { OpenAI } = require('langchain/llms/openai');

// Set up the OpenAI model
const llm = new OpenAI({
  apiKey: process.env.OPENAI_API_KEY,
  temperature: 0.5,
  maxTokens: 200,
});
```

```

### 3. **Prompts**

**Prompts** are structured inputs sent to language models to generate responses. The quality of the prompt is crucial for obtaining relevant outputs from the models. LangChainJS provides tools to build dynamic and complex prompts, allowing you to clearly define the context and expectations for the language model.

A prompt can be simple, like a question, or more complex, containing detailed instructions. LangChainJS also supports prompts that dynamically adapt to input data, enabling the construction of more sophisticated workflows.

Example of a prompt:
```

```javascript
const prompt = "Write a brief summary of the advantages of LangChainJS.";
```

4. **Memory**

Memory in LangChainJS allows for the retention of information across various steps of a chain. This is particularly useful in conversational applications, where the context of a previous conversation needs to be remembered. LangChainJS offers various types of memory, such as short-term or long-term memory, depending on the application's needs.

Example of using memory in a conversation:

```javascript
const { ConversationChain } =
```

```javascript
require('langchain/chains');
const { Memory } = require('langchain/memory');

const memory = new Memory();

// Create a conversation chain with memory
const chain = new ConversationChain({
  llm: llm,
  memory: memory,
});

async function converse() {
  await chain.call("Hello, how are you?");
  await chain.call("What is your favorite color?");

  const response = await chain.call("Do you remember what I asked before?");
```

console.log(response.text); // Memory will recall the previous questions

}

converse();
```


### 5. **Agents**


**Agents** are advanced components that allow a language model to perform specific actions, such as querying external tools or accessing API data. An agent can make decisions based on dynamic input, consult tools, and return a response based on the gathered information.

LangChainJS provides a framework for creating custom agents and linking them to various external tools, such as databases, third-party APIs, or other services.
```

Example of an agent using an external tool:

```javascript
const { OpenAI } = require('langchain/llms/openai');
const { Tool } = require('langchain/tools');
const { AgentExecutor } = require('langchain/agents');

// Define a tool that can be used by the agent
class MyCustomTool extends Tool {
  async call(input) {
    // Implement logic to interact with an API or database
    return `Tool result for input: ${input}`;
  }
}
```

```javascript
const tool = new MyCustomTool();

// Set up the OpenAI model
const llm = new OpenAI({
  apiKey: process.env.OPENAI_API_KEY,
  temperature: 0.7,
});

// Create an agent with the model and tool
const agent = new AgentExecutor({
  llm: llm,
  tools: [tool],
});

// Execute the agent
async function executeAgent() {
  const result = await agent.call("Find information about artificial intelligence.");
```

```
  console.log(result.text);  // Result combining model output and tool
}


executeAgent();
```

6. **Tooling**

Tools in LangChainJS are external resources that agents can use to gather information or perform operations. Tools can be APIs, databases, web services, or even custom functions defined by the developer. LangChainJS provides an interface for easily connecting these tools to agents, allowing them to consult external resources during execution.

Example of using an external API tool:

```javascript
const axios = require('axios');

class WeatherTool extends Tool {
  async call(city) {
    const response = await axios.get(`https://api.weather.com/v3/weather/${city}`);
    return `The weather in ${city} is ${response.data.weather}`;
  }
}

const weatherTool = new WeatherTool();

// Integrate the tool with an agent
const agent = new AgentExecutor({
  llm: llm,
  tools: [weatherTool],
```

```
});

async function checkWeather() {
  const result = await agent.call("What's the weather like in Rome?");
  console.log(result.text);  // Shows Rome's weather
}

checkWeather();
```

Key Components

In addition to the main concepts introduced in the architecture, LangChainJS provides a range of fundamental components that can be combined to build complex workflows. These components include:

1. **LLM Chains**: Connect language models to dynamic prompts and outputs. These chains can be simple or complex depending on the needs.

2. **Prompt Templates**: Allow you to structure and reuse prompts in various contexts, making it easier to create dynamic interactions.

3. **Advanced Memory**: Supports storing complex information for extended sessions or multi-step conversations.

4. **Agent Execution**: Coordinates the use of various external tools by agents to gather data or perform specific operations.

Basic Workflow

The basic workflow of a LangChainJS application can be described in the following steps:

1. **Prompt Input**: The user or application sends a prompt to the language model.

2. **LLM Processing**: The prompt is processed by a language model (e.g., OpenAI GPT or Hugging Face), which returns a response.

3. **Context Memory**: If the application requires context retention (e.g., a conversation), the response and context are saved in memory.

4. **External Tools Usage**: If the agent needs to perform an action requiring external input (e.g., accessing an API), it uses the linked tools to gather the data.

5. **Output to User**: The application returns the result to the user, completing the

cycle.

Example of a workflow:

```javascript
const { OpenAI } = require('langchain/llms/openai');
const { ConversationChain } = require('langchain/chains');
const { Memory } = require('langchain/memory');

// Set up the model and memory
const llm = new OpenAI({ apiKey: process.env.OPENAI_API_KEY });
const memory = new Memory();

// Create a conversation with memory
const chain = new ConversationChain({
```

```
  llm: llm,
  memory: memory,
});


// Execute the conversation
async function startConversation() {
  await chain.call("Hello, how are you?");
  await chain.call("What is your favorite food?");
  const response = await chain.call("Do you remember what I asked before?");
  console.log(response.text);  // Memory will recall previous interactions
}

startConversation();
```

This example illustrates how LangChainJS can orchestrate a complete workflow, from prompt handling to final output, with the ability to maintain context through memory.

3. Using LangChainJS Functions

Data manipulation and the creation of **processing chains** (chains) are core elements. In this detailed guide, we will explore how to use the main features of LangChainJS, providing practical examples for each section: from integrating language models to manipulating data and creating custom processing chains.

Integration with Language Models (LLMs)

Integrating with language models is one of the key features of LangChainJS. Generative language models, like OpenAI GPT-3 and others, are used to generate text, answer questions, complete sentences, or perform any other text-based task. LangChainJS simplifies this integration by offering an interface to interact with various models.

Example 1: Integration with OpenAI GPT

To use a language model like OpenAI GPT, you need to set up API access and create an instance of the model, which can then be used in processing chains.

```javascript
const { OpenAI } = require('langchain/llms/openai');

// Configure the OpenAI language model
const llm = new OpenAI({
  apiKey: process.env.OPENAI_API_KEY, // Set your API key
  temperature: 0.7,            // Adjust model creativity
  maxTokens: 200               // Maximum number of tokens in the output
});
```

```
// Function to generate a response using the GPT model

async function generateResponse(prompt) {

  const response = await llm.generate(prompt);

  console.log(response.text);  // Print the generated response

}


// Example use of the model with a prompt

generateResponse("What are the benefits of artificial intelligence?");
```

In this example, we configured the language model with OpenAI's API key and used it to respond to a prompt. The **temperature** parameter controls the model's creativity: a lower value returns more predictable responses, while a higher value generates more creative ones.

Example 2: Integration with Hugging Face

LangChainJS also supports integration with models hosted on **Hugging Face**, a platform providing access to numerous open-source models.

```javascript
const { HuggingFaceInference } = require('langchain/llms/huggingface');

// Configure the Hugging Face model
const llm = new HuggingFaceInference({
  apiKey: process.env.HUGGINGFACE_API_KEY,
  model: 'gpt2',   // Choose from many models on Hugging Face
});
```

```javascript
// Function to generate a response with the Hugging Face model
async function generateResponse(prompt) {
  const response = await llm.generate(prompt);
  console.log(response.text);  // Print the generated response
}


// Example use with a prompt
generateResponse("What is the future of automation?");
```

In this example, we use an open-source model available on Hugging Face, setting up access through the API and specifying the desired model.

Data Manipulation

A key aspect of LangChainJS is the ability to manipulate data in different formats before sending it to language models or processing it through chains. Data manipulation can include formatting, pre-processing, or dynamic transformations, making the models more efficient or relevant for a specific task.

Example 3: Pre-processing Text

Before sending input to a language model, it's often helpful to format or clean the text. LangChainJS allows for direct text manipulation using standard JavaScript functions or adding custom middleware.

```javascript
// Function to clean text by removing whitespace and special characters
function preprocessText(text) {
  return text.trim().replace(/[^\w\s]/gi, ''); //
```

Removes special characters

}

```
const prompt = preprocessText("   What are the best frameworks for deep learning?!!   ");
generateResponse(prompt);  // Invoke the previous function to generate a response
```

In this example, we remove whitespace and special characters from a prompt before sending it to the language model.

Example 4: Processing Multiple Responses

LangChainJS supports processing complex outputs, such as multiple responses generated from a single model. You can transform and handle this data in various ways.

```javascript
const prompts = [
  "Explain what machine learning is.",
  "What's the difference between AI and ML?",
  "What are the main applications of AI?"
];

// Function to generate multiple responses
async function generateMultipleResponses(prompts) {
  const responses = [];
  for (const prompt of prompts) {
    const response = await llm.generate(prompt);
    responses.push(response.text);  // Add each response to the list
  }
  return responses;
```

```
}

// Execute the function
generateMultipleResponses(prompts).then((responses) => {
  responses.forEach((response, index) => {
    console.log(`Response ${index + 1}: ${response}`);
  });
});
```

Here, we see how to handle multiple prompts in sequence, sending each one to the language model and collecting the responses in an array.

Example 5: Handling Structured Data

LangChainJS also supports integration with

structured data, such as JSON or databases, which can be used as input for language models.

```javascript
const jsonData = {
  title: "AI Application Development",
  description: "A comprehensive guide to building AI-based solutions."
};

// Function to generate a summary based on structured data
async function generateSummaryFromData(data) {
  const prompt = `Summarize the following content: Title: ${data.title}, Description: ${data.description}`;
  const response = await llm.generate(prompt);
  console.log(response.text);  // Print the generated summary
```

}

generateSummaryFromData(jsonData);
```

This example demonstrates how to use structured data in JSON format to generate a summary or response from the language model.

### Creating Processing Chains

One of the most powerful features of LangChainJS is the ability to create **processing chains** (chains), allowing you to link multiple operations and models together. Chains can be simple, like executing operations sequentially, or complex, including branching and the use of external tools or agents.
```

Example 6: Create a Simple Chain

A simple chain might consist of taking an input, processing it through a language model, and returning the result.

```javascript
const { LLMChain } = require('langchain/chains');

// Create a simple chain
const chain = new LLMChain({
  llm: llm,
  prompt: "Explain the benefits of AI in healthcare."
});

// Execute the chain
async function executeChain() {
```

```
    const result = await chain.call();

    console.log(result.text);  // Print the chain result

}


executeChain();
```

In this example, the chain performs a simple step: sending a prompt to the language model and printing the response.

Example 7: Complex Chain with Multiple Steps

More complex chains can include multiple steps or modules chained together. For example, you could have a chain that first extracts information from a text, then uses another model to translate it, and finally sends it via email.

```javascript
const { LLMChain } = require('langchain/chains');

// Define prompts for each step
const promptExtract = "Extract the key points from the following text: ...";
const promptTranslate = "Translate these key points into Italian: ...";

// Create an extraction chain
const extractChain = new LLMChain({
  llm: llm,
  prompt: promptExtract
});
// Create a translation chain
const translateChain = new LLMChain({
  llm: llm,
```

```
  prompt: promptTranslate
});


// Function to execute the chains in sequence
async function executeComplexChain() {
  const extractedData = await extractChain.call();   // Step 1: Extraction
  const translatedData = await translateChain.call({ prompt: extractedData.text });   // Step 2: Translation
  console.log(translatedData.text);   // Print the translation
}


executeComplexChain();
```

In this case, we created a more complex chain that extracts information from a text and then translates that information. The chain is flexible, and each step can be configured or modified.

Example 8: Chain with Memory

LangChainJS also allows creating chains that maintain memory between steps, useful for conversations or workflows where context needs to be maintained.

```javascript
const { ConversationChain } = require('langchain/chains');
const { Memory } = require('langchain/memory');

// Configure the model and memory
const memory = new Memory();
const chain = new ConversationChain({
  llm: llm,
```

```
  memory: memory
});


// Function to execute a chain with memory
async function executeChainWithMemory() {
  await chain.call("Hi, how are you?");
  await chain.call("What's your favorite color?");
  const response = await chain.call("Do you remember what I asked you earlier?");
  console.log(response.text);  // Print the response that uses memory
}


executeChainWithMemory();
```

In this example, memory tracks previous questions, and the model can "remember" past interactions, making the chain more interactive and personalized.

LangChainJS offers a flexible and modular platform for working with language models, allowing developers to create complex, dynamic workflows. Through integration with LLMs, data manipulation, and the creation of processing chains, you can build AI-powered applications that go beyond simple text generation. The provided examples show how LangChainJS can be used to solve real-world problems by integrating multiple processing steps and external tools, maintaining context with memory, and automating complex workflows.

4. Use Cases of LangChainJS

LangChainJS is an advanced JavaScript library that facilitates the development of language model-based applications such as chatbots, virtual assistants, content generation tools, and data analysis solutions. Thanks to its flexible architecture, LangChainJS allows the creation of powerful processing chains that leverage language models to perform specific tasks. In this article, we explore various use cases of LangChainJS, including chatbots, virtual assistants, content generation, and data analysis, with detailed examples.

Chatbots and Virtual Assistants

One of the most common use cases of LangChainJS is the development of chatbots and virtual assistants. LangChainJS provides the necessary tools to build a conversational system that can handle dialogue consistently, maintain memory between sessions, and respond to complex inputs.

Example 1: Customer Support Chatbot

Imagine you want to build a customer support chatbot that answers common questions about a company's products. Using LangChainJS, we can create a conversation that stores the context of previous interactions and responds based on the provided information.

```javascript
const { OpenAI } = require('langchain/llms/openai');

const { ConversationChain } = require('langchain/chains');

const { Memory } = require('langchain/memory');

// Set up the language model and memory
const llm = new OpenAI({ apiKey: process.env.OPENAI_API_KEY });
```

```javascript
const memory = new Memory();

const chain = new ConversationChain({
  llm: llm,
  memory: memory,
});


// Function to start the customer support chatbot
async function startSupportChat() {
  await chain.call("Hello, how can I assist you today?");
  const response1 = await chain.call("What payment methods are available?");
  console.log("Chatbot:", response1.text);


  const response2 = await chain.call("Can I return a product?");
  console.log("Chatbot:", response2.text);
}
```

```
startSupportChat();
```

Description:

In this example, we have set up a customer support chatbot using an OpenAI model that retains the context of the conversation with the help of memory. The chatbot responds to questions related to payment methods and return policies.

Advantages:

- The memory allows the chatbot to "remember" information provided during the conversation, improving dialogue continuity.

- Easily scalable to handle more complex queries or integrations with internal company databases.

Example 2: Personal Virtual Assistant

Another common use case is creating a personal virtual assistant that helps users with daily tasks such as calendar management, creating reminders, or answering personalized questions.

```javascript
const { OpenAI } = require('langchain/llms/openai');

const { ConversationChain } = require('langchain/chains');

const { Memory } = require('langchain/memory');


// Set up the language model and memory
const llm = new OpenAI({ apiKey: process.env.OPENAI_API_KEY });

const memory = new Memory();

const chain = new ConversationChain({
  llm: llm,
  memory: memory,
```

```
});


// Function to start the personal virtual assistant
async function startPersonalAssistant() {
  await chain.call("Good morning, how can I help you today?");
  const response1 = await chain.call("Remind me to call Mario at 3:00 PM.");
  console.log("Assistant:", response1.text);

  const response2 = await chain.call("What do I need to do today?");
  console.log("Assistant:", response2.text);
}

startPersonalAssistant();
```

Description:

In this example, the virtual assistant can respond to commands such as setting reminders or daily tasks. It uses memory to store information about events and tasks, providing personalized responses in future interactions.

Advantages:

- Helps users manage their daily tasks efficiently.

- Memory allows the assistant to maintain context across different sessions.

Content Generation

Content generation is another powerful use case for LangChainJS. Whether for articles, product descriptions, or creative writing, LangChainJS facilitates the automation of the writing process. Using pre-trained language models, it is possible to generate high-quality text on a wide range of topics.

Example 3: Product Description Generation

An example of content generation might be the automated creation of product descriptions for an e-commerce site. LangChainJS can use product details (such as name, features, and benefits) to generate compelling descriptions.

```javascript
const { OpenAI } = require('langchain/llms/openai');


// Set up the OpenAI language model
const llm = new OpenAI({ apiKey: process.env.OPENAI_API_KEY });


// Function to generate a product description
```

```javascript
async function
generateProductDescription(product) {

  const prompt = `Write a captivating description for the following product:

        Name: ${product.name},

        Features: ${product.features.join(', ')},

        Benefits: ${product.benefits.join(', ')}`;


  const response = await llm.generate(prompt);

  console.log("Product description:", response.text);

}


// Example usage

const product = {

  name: "Smartwatch X100",

  features: ["AMOLED display", "Water-resistant", "Health tracking"],
```

```
  benefits: ["Boosts productivity", "Monitors
  physical activity", "Durable and long-lasting"]
};


  generateProductDescription(product);
```

Description:

This example generates a description of the "Smartwatch X100" based on its features and benefits. Using LangChainJS and a language model like OpenAI GPT, the description is fluent and engaging.

Advantages:

- Automates the creation of product descriptions, reducing time and manual effort.

- Can be applied at scale to generate descriptions for thousands of products.

Example 4: Blog Post Generation

LangChainJS can also be used to generate complete blog posts on specific topics, providing valuable support for content creators.

```javascript
const { OpenAI } = require('langchain/llms/openai');

// Set up the OpenAI language model
const llm = new OpenAI({ apiKey: process.env.OPENAI_API_KEY });

// Function to generate a blog post
async function generateBlogPost(topic) {
  const prompt = `Write a 500-word article on the following topic: ${topic}`;
  const response = await llm.generate(prompt);
```

```
  console.log("Generated article:", response.text);

}


// Example usage

generateBlogPost("The importance of cybersecurity in the modern world");
```
```

**Description:**

In this example, LangChainJS automatically generates a 500-word blog post on the importance of cybersecurity. This functionality can be extended to cover different topics, generating content quickly and efficiently.


**Advantages:**

- Speeds up the creation of blog posts on any topic.

- Allows scalable content generation to meet
```

the growing demand for content marketing.

Data Analysis

LangChainJS can also be used for **data analysis** through natural language processing. With the integration of language models, it is possible to analyze large amounts of textual data and obtain meaningful insights.

Example 5: Sentiment Analysis in Social Media

A practical application is sentiment analysis in social media posts to understand how users perceive a product or service.

```javascript
const { OpenAI } = require('langchain/llms/openai');
```

```
// Set up the OpenAI language model
const llm = new OpenAI({ apiKey: process.env.OPENAI_API_KEY });

// Function to analyze the sentiment of a post
async function analyzeSentiment(post) {
  const prompt = `Analyze the sentiment of the following post: ${post}`;
  const response = await llm.generate(prompt);
  console.log("Post sentiment:", response.text);
}

// Example usage
const socialMediaPost = "I love this new smartphone! The features are amazing, and the price is unbeatable.";
analyzeSentiment(socialMediaPost);
```

Description:

In this example, LangChainJS is used to analyze the sentiment of a social media post. The language model identifies whether the tone of the post is positive, negative, or neutral.

Advantages:

- Automates sentiment analysis on social media to monitor customer perceptions.

- Can be integrated with monitoring tools to analyze thousands of posts and comments.

Example 6: Extracting Key Information from Documents

LangChainJS can also be used to extract key information from structured or unstructured text documents, such as business reports, scientific articles, or legal contracts.

```javascript
const { OpenAI } = require('langchain/llms/openai');

// Set up the OpenAI language model
const llm = new OpenAI({ apiKey: process.env.OPENAI_API_KEY });

// Function to extract key information from a document
async function extractKeyInformation(document) {
  const prompt = `Extract key points from the following document: ${document}`;
  const response = await llm.generate(prompt);
  console.log("Key points:", response.text);
}

// Example usage
const document = "Our annual report
```

highlights a 15% revenue growth, with significant gains in the European market.";

extractKeyInformation(document);

```

**Description:**

This example uses LangChainJS to extract key information from a textual document. It can be useful for quickly analyzing long documents and identifying the main points.

**Advantages:**

- Speeds up the analysis of complex documents, saving time.

- Can be applied at scale to automatically analyze business reports, contracts, or legal documents.
```

LangChainJS is an extremely versatile tool, capable of addressing a wide range of use cases that span from creating chatbots and virtual assistants to automating content generation and data analysis. Thanks to its integration with advanced language models and its ability to handle complex data, LangChainJS is a powerful solution for modern applications based on artificial intelligence and natural language processing. By leveraging its tools, it is possible to develop intelligent solutions that improve efficiency and reduce manual workload, delivering significant value across various industries such as customer support, marketing, business analysis, and more.

5.Practical Examples of LangChainJS

In this section, we will walk through several **step-by-step sample projects**, demonstrating how to implement LangChainJS for real-world use cases. Afterward, we will explore **best practices** for optimizing performance, ensuring security, and maintaining efficient code.

LangChainJS Sample Projects (Step-by-Step)

Example 1: FAQ Chatbot with Memory

An FAQ chatbot can respond to frequently asked questions while maintaining a smooth conversation flow using LangChainJS's memory. In this example, we will create a chatbot that uses memory to answer e-commerce questions.

Step 1: Install LangChainJS and OpenAI

First, let's install the necessary libraries.

```bash
npm install langchain openai
```

Step 2: Configure the Language Model and Memory

Set up an OpenAI model to handle response generation and a memory to preserve conversation context.

```javascript
const { OpenAI } = require('langchain/llms/openai');

const { ConversationChain } = require('langchain/chains');
```

```
const { Memory } = require('langchain/memory');

// OpenAI API setup
const llm = new OpenAI({ apiKey: process.env.OPENAI_API_KEY });
const memory = new Memory();

// Create the conversation chain
const chain = new ConversationChain({
  llm: llm,
  memory: memory,
});
```

Step 3: Add Frequently Asked Questions

Now, we can run the chain to simulate a conversation. Let's assume the user asks about shipping and returns.

```javascript
async function faqChatbot() {

  await chain.call("Welcome! How can I assist you today?");

  const response1 = await chain.call("What are the available shipping methods?");

  console.log("Chatbot:", response1.text);


  const response2 = await chain.call("Can I return a product?");

  console.log("Chatbot:", response2.text);


  const response3 = await chain.call("Do you remember what I asked first?");

  console.log("Chatbot:", response3.text);
}
```

```
faqChatbot();
```

Step 4: Run the Project

Now, we can run the chatbot and see how it responds to questions while retaining the context of previous interactions.

Expected result:

- The first response addresses the available shipping methods.

- The second response explains the return process.

- The third response recalls the first question, demonstrating the chatbot's use of memory.

Example 2: Product Description

Generator with LangChainJS

Another practical project is the automatic generation of product descriptions for an online store. This project leverages LangChainJS's content generation capabilities.

Step 1: Install LangChainJS and OpenAI

Ensure the required libraries are installed.

```bash
npm install langchain openai
```

Step 2: Configure the Language Model

Start by configuring the OpenAI model.

```javascript
const { OpenAI } =
require('langchain/llms/openai');


// OpenAI model setup
const llm = new OpenAI({ apiKey:
process.env.OPENAI_API_KEY });
```

Step 3: Create the Generation Function

Create a function that takes the product details (name, features, benefits) and generates a description.

```javascript
async function
generateProductDescription(product) {

  const prompt = `Write a detailed description for the following product:
```

```
        Name: ${product.name},
        Features: ${product.features.join(', ')},
        Benefits: ${product.benefits.join(', ')}`;

  const response = await llm.generate(prompt);
  console.log("Product Description:", response.text);
}
```

Step 4: Execute the Function with a Sample Product

Run the description generator with a sample product.

```javascript
const product = {
```

```
  name: "Smartwatch X200",

  features: ["AMOLED Display", "Built-in GPS", "Sleep Monitoring"],

  benefits: ["Improve your lifestyle", "Perfect for athletes", "Elegant and modern design"]
};


generateProductDescription(product);
```

Expected result:

The function will return an appealing and well-structured description of the "Smartwatch X200," which can be used on an e-commerce website.

Example 3: Social Media Comment Sentiment Analysis

In this project, we will use LangChainJS to analyze social media comments and determine the sentiment (positive, negative, or neutral) of the comments.

Step 1: Install LangChainJS and OpenAI

```bash
npm install langchain openai
```

Step 2: Configure the Language Model

Set up the OpenAI model to analyze sentiment.

```javascript
const { OpenAI } = require('langchain/llms/openai');
```

```
// OpenAI API setup

const llm = new OpenAI({ apiKey: process.env.OPENAI_API_KEY });
```

Step 3: Create the Sentiment Analysis Function

Write a function that takes a comment as input and returns the sentiment analysis.

```javascript
async function analyzeSentiment(comment) {

  const prompt = `Analyze the sentiment of the following comment: "${comment}" and state whether it is positive, negative, or neutral.`;

  const response = await llm.generate(prompt);
  console.log("Comment Sentiment:",
```

```
    response.text);
}
```

Step 4: Run the Function with a Sample Comment

Execute the function with a sample comment.

```javascript
const comment = "I love the new website design! It's much easier to use.";
analyzeSentiment(comment);
```

Expected result:

LangChainJS will return the sentiment of the comment (positive in this case), helping to quickly assess user opinions on social media.

Best Practices for Using LangChainJS

LangChainJS is a powerful tool, but to get the most out of it, it is important to follow some best practices to optimize performance, ensure security, and maintain code efficiently.

1. Performance Optimization

Using language models can be resource-intensive, so it's important to adopt strategies to optimize performance.

Response Caching:

- For repetitive tasks like answering FAQs or generating standard content, cache the responses to reduce the number of API calls.

```javascript
const cache = new Map();
```

```js
async function cachedGenerate(prompt) {
  if (cache.has(prompt)) {
    return cache.get(prompt);
  }
  const response = await llm.generate(prompt);
  cache.set(prompt, response);
  return response;
}
```

Optimizing API Requests:

- Frequent API calls can be costly in terms of latency and expenses. Use batching or reduce the frequency of API calls when possible.

Context Size Management:

- Limit the amount of information passed to

the model to avoid exceeding context limits, as it can slow down processing.

2. Application Security

Security is crucial when developing applications that interact with sensitive data or use third-party APIs.

API Key Protection:

- Never expose API keys directly in frontend code. Use environment variables or secure backend services to handle the keys.

```bash
// .env
OPENAI_API_KEY=your-api-key-here
```

Input Validation:

- If the application accepts user input (e.g., in a chatbot), validate and sanitize the input to avoid injection attacks or other vulnerabilities.

Authorization Management:

- Implement appropriate authentication and authorization mechanisms to protect access to critical application functions.

3. Code Maintenance

To keep LangChainJS code well-structured and easy to maintain, follow these best practices.

Modularity:

- Break the code into smaller, reusable modules. For example, separate language generation logic from user response handling.

Automated Testing:

- Write automated tests to ensure functions continue working correctly during updates or code changes.

```javascript
const assert = require('assert');

async function testGenerateProductDescription() {
  const product = { name: "Smartwatch", features: ["GPS"], benefits: ["Precise tracking"] };
  const description = await generateProductDescription(product);
  assert(description.includes("Smartwatch"), "Description should contain the product name");
}

testGenerateProductDescription();
```

Documentation:

- Keep documentation up to date to facilitate future development.

6. Integrating LangChainJS with Other Tools and Libraries

LangChainJS is a powerful library known for its flexibility and ability to integrate with other tools and libraries to build advanced AI applications. In this guide, we'll explore how to integrate LangChainJS with **RESTful APIs**, **databases and storage**, and **UI frameworks**. We'll also cover how to troubleshoot common errors with detailed solutions.

Integrating LangChainJS with RESTful APIs

Integrating with RESTful APIs is essential for making language models and processing chains available to other applications. You can create endpoints that use LangChainJS to process requests and return responses.

Example: Building a RESTful API with

LangChainJS and Express

1. **Step 1: Install Dependencies**

First, install **Express**, a minimalist framework for building web servers, along with LangChainJS.

```bash
npm install express langchain openai
```

2. **Step 2: Set Up Express Server**

Create an Express server that handles a POST request to generate responses using LangChainJS.

```javascript
```

```javascript
const express = require('express');
const { OpenAI } = require('langchain/llms/openai');
require('dotenv').config();

const app = express();
app.use(express.json());

// Configure OpenAI via LangChainJS
const llm = new OpenAI({ apiKey: process.env.OPENAI_API_KEY });

// POST endpoint for text generation
app.post('/generate', async (req, res) => {
  const { prompt } = req.body;

  if (!prompt) {
    return res.status(400).send({ error: "Prompt not provided" });
```

```js
  }

  try {
    const response = await llm.generate(prompt);
    res.status(200).send({ result: response.text });
  } catch (error) {
    res.status(500).send({ error: "Text generation error" });
  }
});

// Start the server
const PORT = process.env.PORT || 3000;
app.listen(PORT, () => {
  console.log(`Server running on port ${PORT}`);
});
```

```

3. **Step 3: Test the API**

You can test the functionality by sending a POST request with a prompt to the server:

```bash
curl -X POST http://localhost:3000/generate -H "Content-Type: application/json" -d '{"prompt": "Explain the theory of relativity"}'
```

Expected Result:

The API will return a response generated by the OpenAI model, such as an explanation of the theory of relativity.

Benefits of Integrating with RESTful APIs
```

- **Accessibility:** Other systems can easily interact with your AI application through simple HTTP calls.

- **Scalability:** You can deploy the server in scalable production environments like AWS, Heroku, or Google Cloud.

Integrating with Databases and Storage

Database integration is crucial when you need to store input, results, or conversation contexts generated by LangChainJS. You can use relational databases like MySQL or NoSQL databases like MongoDB to store and retrieve data.

Example: Using MongoDB with LangChainJS

1. **Step 1: Install Dependencies**

Install MongoDB and its client library, **Mongoose**.

```bash
npm install mongoose langchain openai
```

2. **Step 2: Configure MongoDB**

Connect MongoDB to your application and configure a schema to store prompts and generated responses.

```javascript
const mongoose = require('mongoose');
const { OpenAI } =
```

```javascript
require('langchain/llms/openai');

// Connect to MongoDB
mongoose.connect('mongodb://localhost:27017/langchainDB', { useNewUrlParser: true, useUnifiedTopology: true });

// Define schema and model
const promptSchema = new mongoose.Schema({
  prompt: String,
  response: String,
});

const PromptModel = mongoose.model('Prompt', promptSchema);

// Configure LangChainJS with OpenAI
const llm = new OpenAI({ apiKey: process.env.OPENAI_API_KEY });
```

```javascript
// Function to generate and save a response
async function generateAndSave(promptText) {
  const response = await llm.generate(promptText);

  // Save the prompt and response to the database
  const newPrompt = new PromptModel({
    prompt: promptText,
    response: response.text,
  });

  await newPrompt.save();
  console.log("Generated and saved response:", response.text);
}
```

3. **Step 3: Run the Function**

Call the function with a sample prompt.

```javascript
generateAndSave("What is blockchain?");
```

Expected Result:

The prompt and response will be saved in the MongoDB database, and you can access them later for analysis or reuse.

Benefits of Database Integration

- **Persistence:** You can permanently store prompts and responses, allowing future analysis.

- **Scalability:** Using a database enables handling large amounts of data generated by the AI application.

- **Retrievability:** You can resume past conversations or interactions, which is useful for chatbots or customer support applications.

Integrating with UI Frameworks

To create an interactive user interface that uses LangChainJS, you can integrate it with frontend frameworks like **React** or **Vue.js**. This allows users to interact directly with language models through a smooth UI.

Example: Integrating LangChainJS with React

1. **Step 1: Set Up a React Project**

Start by setting up a React project:

```bash
npx create-react-app langchain-react
cd langchain-react
npm install axios
```

2. **Step 2: Create a Backend Express Server with LangChainJS**

We'll use the RESTful API created earlier and connect it to the React frontend.

3. **Step 3: Frontend Integration in React**

In the React component, use **Axios** to

send requests to the LangChainJS server.

```javascript
import React, { useState } from 'react';
import axios from 'axios';

function App() {
  const [prompt, setPrompt] = useState('');
  const [response, setResponse] = useState('');

  const handleSubmit = async (e) => {
    e.preventDefault();
    const res = await axios.post('http://localhost:3000/generate', { prompt });
    setResponse(res.data.result);
  };

  return (
```

```jsx
    <div className="App">
      <h1>LangChainJS Chatbot</h1>
      <form onSubmit={handleSubmit}>
        <input
          type="text"
          value={prompt}
          onChange={(e) => setPrompt(e.target.value)}
          placeholder="Enter your question..."
        />
        <button type="submit">Submit</button>
      </form>
      {response && <p>Response: {response}</p>}
    </div>
  );
}

export default App;
```

```

4. **Step 4: Run the Application**

Start the Express backend and the React frontend, then interact with the chatbot directly from the React interface.

```bash
npm start   # For React
```

Expected Result:

Users can enter prompts into the React frontend and receive generated responses from the language model in real time.

Benefits of UI Framework Integration
```

- **User Interaction:** You can create intuitive user experiences that allow interaction with language models.

- **Responsiveness:** Interfaces built with React or other frameworks are dynamic and support real-time updates.

- **Customization:** You can easily tailor the user experience and interface to suit various application contexts.

Troubleshooting

Common Errors and Solutions

When developing with LangChainJS, you may encounter some common errors. Here's how to address them.

1. Error: "Invalid API key"

Description: This error occurs when the API key provided to LangChainJS is incorrect or not set.

Solution: Ensure your API key is correctly set and that the `.env` file contains the correct key.

```bash
OPENAI_API_KEY=your-api-key
```

Also, ensure you've loaded environment variables correctly in the code.

```javascript
require('dotenv').config();
```

2. Error: "Model not supported"

Description: LangChainJS may return an error if the requested model is unsupported or misconfigured.

Solution: Check the OpenAI documentation to ensure the model you're trying to use is available and configured correctly.

```javascript
const llm = new OpenAI({ model: 'text-davinci-003', apiKey: process.env.OPENAI_API_KEY });
```

3. Error: "Context limit exceeded"

Description: This error occurs when the text sent to the model exceeds the context limit (maximum token length).

Solution: Reduce the length of the prompt or split the text into smaller parts. You can also use memory functions to retain some context without sending it all at once.

```javascript
const truncatedPrompt = prompt.slice(0, 2000); // Trim the prompt to a safe length
```

4. Error: "Database connection failed"

Description: This error may occur when your code cannot connect to the database.

Solution: Ensure MongoDB (or the database you're using) is running and that the connection credentials are correct.

```javascript
mongoose.connect('mongodb://localhost:27017/langchainDB', { useNewUrlParser: true, useUnifiedTopology: true });
```

5. Performance Issue: High API Call Latency

Description: API calls to the model may be slow, causing delays in request processing.

Solution: Use **caching** techniques or reduce the frequency of requests. You may also consider upgrading to a higher API plan for faster response times.

With these integrations and troubleshooting techniques, you can build advanced and robust applications using LangChainJS and ensure they run efficiently and securely in production.

7.Glossary of LangChainJS

1. **LangChain**

LangChain is a library that facilitates interaction with large language models, such as those provided by OpenAI (e.g., GPT-3, GPT-4), by integrating pre-trained models and data processing pipelines. LangChain's primary focus is the creation of complex workflows that connect various language models and tools to manage conversations, generate content, solve problems, and more.

---

2. **Language Model (LLM)**

Definition:

A **Large Language Model (LLM)** is an algorithm trained on vast amounts of text data to understand and generate natural language. These models are the foundation of many natural language processing (NLP) services used in LangChainJS.

Example:

In LangChainJS, you can use an LLM to generate text or answer questions.

```javascript
const { OpenAI } = require('langchain/llms/openai');

const llm = new OpenAI({ apiKey: process.env.OPENAI_API_KEY });

llm.generate("What is the theory of relativity?").then(response => {

   console.log(response);

});
```

---

3. **Prompt**

Definition:

A **prompt** is the input text provided to the language model. It serves as the basis for generating a response. The quality of the prompt directly influences the quality of the response generated.

Example:

```javascript
const prompt = "Explain the theory of relativity in simple terms.";
const response = await llm.generate(prompt);
console.log(response.text);
```

---

4. **Chain**

Definition:

A **chain** is a sequence of operations or steps that can be combined to build complex workflows. Chains in LangChainJS allow you to link multiple models or processes, enabling more advanced interactions.

Example:

A chain might combine a language model with a search function to answer more complex questions.

```javascript
const { LLMChain } = require('langchain');

const chain = new LLMChain({ llm, promptTemplate });

const result = await chain.run({ input: "What is the capital of France?" });
```

---

5. **Prompt Template**

Definition:

A **prompt template** is a predefined structure that allows dynamic generation of prompts by inserting variables to obtain more specific responses.

Example:

```javascript
const { PromptTemplate } = require('langchain/prompts');

const template = new PromptTemplate("Explain {topic} in simple terms.");

const prompt = template.fill({ topic: "blockchain" });
```

```
console.log(prompt); // "Explain blockchain in simple terms."
```

---

6. **Memory**

Definition:

Memory in LangChainJS refers to the ability to retain and manage information between consecutive interactions with a language model. This is especially useful in conversational applications (like chatbots), where it is necessary to maintain the context of the conversation.

Example:

```javascript
const { ConversationChain } = require('langchain/chains');
```

```
const conversation = new ConversationChain({ llm });

await conversation.memory.addMessage({ role: "user", content: "Who is Albert Einstein?" });

const response = await conversation.run({ message: "What was his most important discovery?" });

console.log(response);
```

---

7. **Retrieval-Augmented Generation (RAG)**

Definition:

RAG refers to an approach that combines text generation with retrieving relevant information from a database or an external knowledge source. This technique enhances the accuracy of responses.

Example:

```javascript
const { OpenAI, DatabaseRetriever } = require('langchain');

const llm = new OpenAI({ apiKey: process.env.OPENAI_API_KEY });

const retriever = new DatabaseRetriever({ databaseURL: "mongodb://localhost:27017" });

const chain = new LLMChain({ llm, retriever });

const result = await chain.run({ query: "What did Einstein discover?" });
```

---

8. **Toolkit**

Definition:

A **toolkit** in LangChainJS is a collection of tools that work together to perform specific operations. Tools can include language models, text manipulation processes, or interfaces to retrieve data.

---

9. **Output Parser**

Definition:

An **output parser** is a function or module that interprets and transforms the model's output into a specific format. This can be useful for extracting structured responses from language models.

Example:

```javascript
```

```
const parser = (response) => {

  return response.text.split("\n").map(line => line.trim());

};

const result = await llm.generate("Give me a list of tropical fruits.");

const parsedOutput = parser(result);

console.log(parsedOutput); // ["Mango", "Papaya", "Pineapple", ...]
```

---

10. **Callback**

Definition:

A **callback** is a function that is called at the end of a process or when an event occurs. LangChainJS uses callbacks to handle results and responses, enabling asynchronous workflows.

---

11. **Agent**

Definition:

An **agent** is an advanced component that makes decisions about which action to take based on a set of available tools and the current context. Agents can choose between different language models, query databases, or call APIs.

Example:

```javascript
const { ZeroShotAgent } = require('langchain/agents');

const agent = new ZeroShotAgent({ tools: [llm, retriever] });
```

```
const result = await agent.run("Search for information on Albert Einstein.");
```

---

12. **Tool**

Definition:

A **tool** in LangChainJS is a specific module or functionality that the agent can use to perform tasks, such as calling an API, conducting searches, or generating text.

---

13. **Schema**

Definition:

A **schema** in LangChainJS defines the structure of data or context used by a chain or language model. Schemas help structure and organize data more efficiently.

---

14. **Conversational Memory**

Definition:

Conversational memory keeps track of past interactions in a conversation to maintain context and provide more coherent responses in future interactions.

Example:

```javascript
const { ConversationChain } = require('langchain/chains');

const conversation = new ConversationChain({ llm });
```

```
await
conversation.memory.addMessage({ role:
"user", content: "What is relativity?" });

await
conversation.memory.addMessage({ role:
"user", content: "How does it apply in daily
life?" });

const response = await
conversation.run({ message: "Explain its
connection with GPS." });
```

---

15. **Embedding**

Definition:

An **embedding** is a vector representation of text that allows language models to calculate similarities and semantic relationships between phrases or words. Embeddings are used for information retrieval or to improve model responses.

Example:

```javascript
const { OpenAIEmbeddings } = require('langchain/embeddings');

const embeddings = new OpenAIEmbeddings({ apiKey: process.env.OPENAI_API_KEY });

const vector = await embeddings.embedText("What is the theory of relativity?");

console.log(vector);
```

---

16. **Text Splitter**

Definition:

A **text splitter** is a module that divides large portions of text into smaller fragments, making it easier for the language model to process long texts.

Example:

```javascript
const { RecursiveCharacterTextSplitter } = require('langchain/text_splitter');

const splitter = new RecursiveCharacterTextSplitter({ chunkSize: 500 });

const chunks = splitter.splitText("This is a very long text...");

console.log(chunks);
```

---

17. **Document**

Definition:

A **document** in LangChainJS is an entity that represents a piece of structured text, useful for processing or retrieving information.

---

18. **Query**

Definition:

A **query** is a specific request made to the model or database to obtain a response or retrieve data.

---

19. **Cognitive Load**

Definition:

Cognitive load refers to the complexity of a chain or workflow. Optimizing cognitive load means simplifying model interactions by reducing the complexity of the prompt or context.

This LangChainJS glossary provides an overview of key terms and concepts for working with the library. With the help of practical examples, you can better understand LangChainJS's functionalities and architecture, facilitating the development of complex applications based on language models.

Index

1. Introduction pg.4

2. Fundamental Concepts pg.17

3. Using LangChainJS Functions pg.36

4. Use Cases of LangChainJS pg,54

5. Practical Examples of LangChainJS pg.72

6. Integrating LangChainJS with Other Tools and Libraries pg.90

7. Glossary of LangChainJS pg.111

www.ingramcontent.com/pod-product-compliance
Lightning Source LLC
Chambersburg PA
CBHW050306230526
45471CB00005B/2046